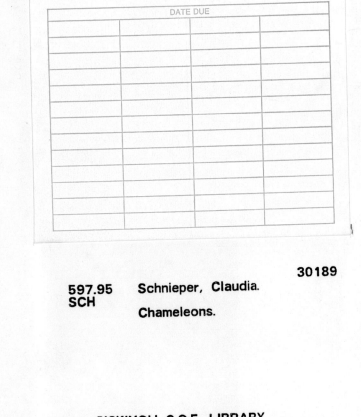

Chameleons

Chamaeleo dilepis

Chameleons

by Claudia Schnieper/photographs by Max Meier

A Carolrhoda Nature Watch Book

 Carolrhoda Books, Inc./Minneapolis

*Thanks to James E. Gerholdt, The Remarkable Reptiles,
for his assistance with this book.*

This edition first published 1989 by Carolrhoda Books, Inc.
Original edition copyright © 1986 by Kinderbuchverlag Reich Luzern
AG, Lucerne, Switzerland, under the title DAS CHAMÄLEON.
Translated from the German by Betmar Languages. Adapted by
Carolrhoda Books, Inc.
All additional material supplied for this edition ©1989 by
Carolrhoda Books, Inc.

LIBRARY OF CONGRESS CATALOGING-IN-PUBLICATION DATA

Schnieper, Claudia.
    [Chamäleon. English]
    Chameleons / by Claudia Schnieper : photographs by Max Meier
      p.   cm.
    Translation of: Das Chamäleon.
    "A Carolrhoda nature watch book"
    Includes index.
    Summary: Discusses the physical characteristics, behavior, and
life cycle of the lizard known for its ability to change its color.
    ISBN 0-87614-341-9 (lib. bdg.)
    1. Chameleons—Juvenile literature. [1. Chameleons.] I. Meier,
Max, ill. II. Title.
QL666.L23S313   1989   88-37646
597.95—dc19   CIP
                                        AC

Manufactured in the United States of America

  2 3 4 5 6 7 8 9 10 99 98 97 96 95 94 93 92 91 90 89

The scientific name of the two chameleons shown here is *Chamaeleo fischeri*. Like many of their relatives, they have no English names.

The chameleon is an amazing animal. Its eyes can look in opposite directions at the same time. Its feet can grip like powerful tongs. A chameleon can hang onto a tree branch with its tail and use its tongue as a long-range weapon. To add to all this, chameleons can change the color of their skins. In minutes, they can go from green to brown or break out in bright stripes and spots.

What kind of animal can do all these remarkable things? Let's take a closer look at chameleons and find out what they are really like.

Chamaeleo chamaeleon

Chameleons (kuh-MEAL-yuhns) are lizards, scale-covered animals related to snakes, crocodiles, turtles, and tuataras. Like their relatives, lizards belong to the scientific group of **reptiles**.

Reptiles have many different characteristics. One of the important things they have in common is the way their body temperatures are regulated. Chameleons and other reptiles are **ecto-therms (ECK-toh-therms)**, animals whose temperatures are controlled from outside their bodies. In sunshine or warm weather, their temperatures rise. When reptiles are in a cool environment, their temperatures fall. Mammals and birds are **endotherms (EHN-doh-therms)**. They have temperatures controlled from within their bodies.

Like other lizards, most chameleons live in warm climates where there is plenty of sunshine to keep their bodies working. Many kinds of chameleons are found in Africa south of the Sahara Desert and on the large island of Madagascar, near the southeastern coast of Africa. A few chameleons live in the Middle East, southern Asia, and southern Europe. The European chameleon, shown on these two pages, comes from the southern part of Spain, near the Mediterranean Sea. Wherever they live, most chameleons make their homes in trees and bushes.

A lizard found in South and Central America and in the southeastern United States is sometimes called a chameleon. It is not actually a true chameleon but a distant relative known as the **anole (uh-NOH-lee)**. Like chameleons, anoles can change the colors of their skins.

8

Chamaeleo quadricornis

There are at least 85 different species, or kinds, of true chameleons. The largest are about 2½ feet (about 76 centimeters) long, including their tails. There are also some very small chameleons that measure only ¾ inch (about 2 centimeters) in length.

The different kinds of chameleons have many strange decorations on their scaly bodies. Some chameleons have raised crests on their backs and tails. Others have helmet-shaped heads or flaps and spikes hanging under their chins.

Horns are common ornaments on some kinds of chameleons. The chameleon shown here has four horns on its head. Other species have one, two, or three horns, or no horns at all.

Chamaeleo senegalensis

Chamaeleo dilepis

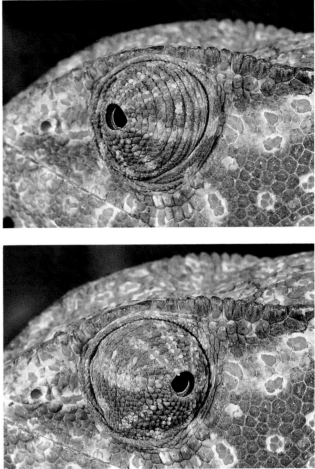

The eyes of a chameleon are different from the eyes of other lizards. In fact, they are different from the eyes of most kinds of animals.

A chameleon's eyes bulge out on either side of its head. They are almost completely covered by cone-shaped lids. There is only a small opening in each lid, located over the pupil of the eye.

When a chameleon wants to look at something, it rotates its whole eye in order to focus on the object. Each eye can be moved independently. While the left eye looks down at an insect on the ground, the right eye can be turned upward to watch a bird in the sky.

A chameleon can also turn both eyes forward to focus on the same object. This makes it possible for chameleons to have **binocular (bih-NOCK-you-luhr) vision**, as humans do. Many other animals with eyes on the sides of their heads can only see a separate image with each eye.

Not only do chameleons have unusual eyes, but they also have very special feet. A chameleon's feet are particularly suited for its life among the branches of trees and shrubs.

Most other lizards live on the ground. They have long, thin toes useful for scurrying from place to place. Chameleons have toes that are fused, or joined, in two bunches to form a kind of clamp.

On the front feet, two toes are bunched together on the outside of each foot. Three toes form a bunch on the inside. The hind feet have the opposite arrangement—three toes on the outside, and two on the inside. Strong claws at the ends of the toes help a chameleon to get a powerful grip on a branch.

A chameleon's grip is so powerful that the animal can hang upside down

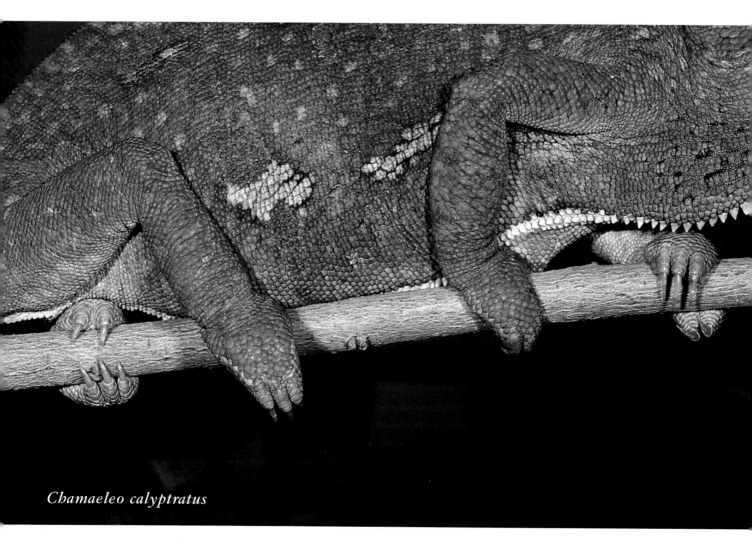

Chamaeleo calyptratus

12

Chamaeleo gracilis

beneath a branch while holding on with its feet. Chameleons also sleep in the branches of trees, depending on their remarkable feet to keep them from falling.

Because a chameleon's feet are so well suited for life in the trees, they aren't very practical for other uses. Compared to most lizards, chameleons are clumsy on the ground. Their clamp-shaped feet are not made for running. Most chameleons stay on the ground only long enough to move from tree to tree (below) or to lay their eggs.

Chamaeleo africanus

Chamaeleo dilepis

Chamaeleo montium

If a chameleon somehow loses its foothold on a tree branch, it can still hang on with its tail. Chameleon tails are **prehensile (pree-HEN-sihl)**. This means that they can wrap around objects and grip them, just like the tails of many monkeys. When a chameleon's tail is not wrapped around a branch, it is usually kept curled up in a flat coil.

Very few other lizards have prehensile tails. But many lizards can do something with their tails that chameleons can't do. They can separate them from their bodies. When a **predator** grabs a lizard by its tail, the tail will often break off at a special weak point. The predator is left with a wiggling tail, while the rest of the lizard escapes. Within a few months, the lizard will grow a new tail.

Chameleons can't drop their tails, and they can't grow new ones. If a chameleon loses its tail in an accident, it will be tailless for the rest of its life.

All of a chameleon's unusual features —tail, eyes, and feet—are put into use when the animal hunts for food. Most chameleons eat grasshoppers, flies, and other insects. They look for their **prey** among the branches of trees.

A hunting chameleon waits quietly on a branch. Its eyes swivel around constantly, watching for a meal. When the lizard spots a insect, it creeps toward it, moving each foot carefully from one hold to another. Then the chameleon gets a good grip on the branch with its feet and tail and prepares to attack.

The tool that a chameleon uses to capture food is its long tube-shaped tongue. This amazing tongue is often as long as the lizard's body. When it is not in use, it is bunched up inside the mouth, something like a sleeve pushed up on an arm. The "arm" is a piece of cartilage called the **hyoid (HI-oyd) bone**, which extends into the mouth from the throat bones.

A chameleon's tongue is surrounded by strong muscles that can shoot it out of the animal's mouth at incredible speed. Here is what happens. . . .

With its eyes fixed on its prey, the chameleon takes aim and fires its long-range weapon. In the photograph on the upper left, you can see the club-shaped end of the tongue just coming out of its mouth.

The tongue hits its target, a grasshopper (lower left). Sticky mucus on the end holds the struggling insect as the chameleon pulls its meal into its mouth (upper right). Powerful muscles gather the tongue in and push it back over the hyoid bone.

At the end of a successful hunt, the chameleon crunches up the grasshopper with its small teeth (lower right). Chameleons are very good hunters and almost never miss their targets.

Chamaeleo gracilis

Chameleons have many remarkable features. But most people remember only one thing about these lizards—their ability to change colors.

Color changing is not special to chameleons. Many animals, including fish, frogs, and other lizards, have the ability to change the color of their skins. Research has shown that these changes are usually produced by movements of tiny particles of coloring materials called **pigments (PIG-muhnts)**.

Chameleons have several kinds of pigments located within different cells in their skin. The pigment that is responsible for most color changes is **melanin** **(MEL-uh-nihn)**. This is a dark substance contained in cells known as **melanophores (muh-LAN-uh-fores)**.

When the melanin particles are concentrated in one place inside the melanophores, the bright yellow and blue pigments in other skin cells can be seen. Then a chameleon's skin usually looks green, like the animal shown above.

When the dark melanin spreads out within the melanophores, it covers up some of the other pigment cells. This causes the skin to appear brownish or even black (opposite). Other movements of different pigments can create stripes and spots of color.

Chamaeleo rudis

Chamaeleo calyptratus

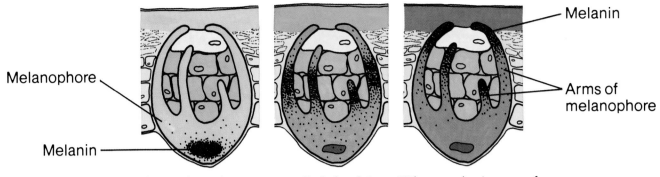

Melanophore

Melanin

Melanin

Arms of melanophore

Melanophores have long arms called dendrites. When melanin spreads out into these arms, it covers up some of the colors in other pigment cells.

The movement of pigments produces color changes, but what makes the pigments move? Can chameleons choose to move their pigments in order to create different colors?

Chameleons cannot "decide" to change the color of their skins. The changes are controlled automatically by their **hormones** and nervous systems. They often take place in response to external conditions such as temperature and amount of light. For example, many chameleons become light in color when they are in a warm environment. They turn darker when temperatures are cool.

Another important influence on a chameleon's color is the animal's mood. Chameleons that are afraid or upset often change colors rapidly, becoming darker or developing spots. Different combinations of colors and patterns reflect other moods such as calmness or anger.

Scientists used to think that color changes helped chameleons to blend into their environment. They believed that the lizards changed to green or brown to match the leaves or branches around them. Studies now show that this does not seem to be true. Often a chameleon will wear a dark color even though it is standing in front of green leaves. In the dark of the night, many chameleons change to a light color. In general, color changes don't seem to have much to do with camouflage.

Scientists still don't understand all the details of color changing in chameleons and other lizards. But they know that such changes are an important part of the animals' lives.

The photographs on these two pages show the different colors displayed by just one species of chameleon, the flap-necked chameleon. They demonstrate how color can express a chameleon's mood and condition.

On the upper left, you can see a female flap-necked chameleon defending her territory against another chameleon. Her stripes and spots, as well as her open mouth, show that she is in a fighting mood.

The female on the lower left has mated and is now expecting young. Her markings tell males of her species to stay away.

On the upper right is a female showing a very dark color. She was the loser in a contest with another chameleon. Her color probably reflects fear and anger.

The male at the lower right is looking for a mate. He has raised the flaps on the back of his neck and spread his throat flap to attract females of his species. His yellow stripes add to the impressive display.

The outer layer of a chameleon's skin is made of a colorless material called **keratin (KEHR-uh-tihn)**. Unlike human skin, this material does not expand as the animal grows. Chameleons, like other reptiles, must replace their outer skin layers from time to time.

When a chameleon is getting ready to **molt** its skin, it sits quietly on a branch. Its body looks swollen, and its color is dull and pale (upper left). Soon the outer layer of skin begins to split (middle left).

Snakes lose their old skins in one piece, but a chameleon's skin comes off in sections. The lizard uses its feet to pull off the pieces of skin (lower left). Underneath, a new layer of keratin has already developed. This new skin layer is looser and will give the chameleon room to grow.

The flap-necked chameleon in the photograph on the opposite page is in the middle of molting. Where the old skin has peeled off, you can see the lizard's bright colors shining through the new layer of keratin.

Chamaeleo dilepis

Flap-necked chameleons make their homes in Africa, like so many of their relatives. They are common in South Africa, where they live in forested areas. Adult flap-necks are about 6 inches (15 centimeters) in length, which is an average size for many chameleons. The common name of this species comes from the flaps behind their heads, which can be raised or lowered. Like most chameleons, flap-necked chameleons spend almost all their lives among the branches of trees and bushes.

Chamaeleo montium

The mountain chameleon shown here lives in the rain forest on the slopes of Mount Cameroon in West Africa (opposite). It makes its home in the dense undergrowth beneath the giant trees. Here the mountain chameleon hides from predators like snakes and birds by keeping perfectly still.

Amid the green trees, each mountain chameleon has its own small territory, sometimes only a few branches. It has a special place in its territory where it returns each night to sleep. The chameleon marks the spot with saliva and probably finds it by smell.

Chameleons are not social animals. Each one lives by itself and tries to keep other chameleons out of its territory. When it is time for mating, however, male and female chameleons have to give up their solitary lives.

29

The photograph above shows a male mountain chameleon that is ready to mate. His bright colors and spots express his mood. The male has found a female mountain chameleon, but there is another male that is also trying to win her as a mate. There may be a battle between the two rivals.

Male mountain chameleons have two long horns that they use in fights.

They also use sounds and visual signals to defeat their opponents. A male that is ready to fight opens his mouth wide and hisses loudly (opposite left). He stretches his body up high and turns sideways to his rival. In this way, he looks bigger and more threatening. If the other male is not scared away by this display, then the two chameleons will fight.

30

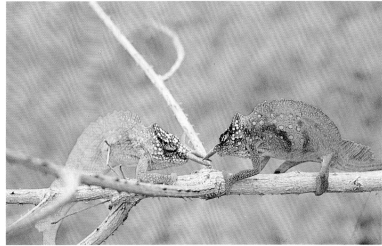

The photographs on the right show a fight between two male mountain chameleons. The lighter-colored animal in the picture is the attacker. The darker chameleon is trying to defend himself, but he is weaker than his opponent.

As the battle continues, the weaker male becomes darker and darker. His change in color indicates that he is angry and afraid. Finally, he gives up and attempts to hide from his attacker by hanging under the tree branch.

The chameleon on the left is the winner in this battle. He will mate with the female—if she is willing to accept him.

Chamaeleo dilepis

On the opposite page is another male chameleon that is looking for a mate. This is a flap-necked male, and he is dressed in a very light color for the occasion.

In the photograph on the upper right, the male has found a female flap-neck. Her green color indicates that she is in a good mood and will probably allow the male to stay in her territory.

The male flap-neck uses different signals to encourage the female to mate with him. He moves toward her slowly, hissing and swaying his body from side to side. When the male reaches out to touch the female, her color gradually changes to a light brown. This seems to be a sign that she will not fight with him but will accept him as a mate.

When the two chameleons mate (above), the male's sperm cells pass into the female's reproductive system. There the sperm cells will unite with the female's egg cells. With this union, new little chameleons will start to develop inside the female's body.

Some male and female chameleons stay together for a few days at mating time. But soon both return to their solitary lives.

A female flap-neck that is expecting young changes to a dark color dotted with many spots (opposite above). This pattern tells males of her species that she is not available as a mate. If a male ignores the message and comes near her, she will drive him away.

In the photograph on the right, a pregnant flap-necked female is facing a male flap-neck. He has puffed himself up to look important, but she is letting him know that his presence is not welcome.

Inside the female's body, new life is growing. At this stage, the developing baby chameleons are called **embryos (EHM-bree-ohs)**. Each embryo is enclosed inside a soft egg shell.

When the female flap-neck is ready to lay her eggs, she comes down from the trees. Like most chameleons, she lays her eggs on the ground. With her hind legs, she digs a hole big enough to hold her body. Then she climbs into the hole and deposits her eggs in it.

After covering her eggs with dirt, the female returns to the trees. Her job as a parent is finished.

Buried in the ground, the chameleon eggs slowly develop. The covering of dirt keeps them warm and moist. Inside the shells, the embryos are nourished by the egg yolks, which provide the food they need to grow.

Chameleon eggs develop for different lengths of time, depending on the species of chameleon. Flap-necked embryos usually take around 10 months to complete their growth. Then the eggs are ready to hatch.

Under the ground, each baby chameleon cuts its egg shell open with a special **egg tooth** in the front of its mouth. Then it struggles to the surface through the loose soil. The newly hatched flap-neck is tiny, only 1½ inches (about 4 centimeters) in length. Blinking its eyes in the bright sunlight, the little animal quickly climbs into the trees.

Not all the buried eggs hatch. Some may have been damaged by too much heat or cold. Predators or disease can also destroy chameleon eggs.

But at first, their aim is not as good as adult chameleons. They need practice before they become expert shots.

Just like adult chameleons, the babies do not get along well together. Early in their lives, they begin fighting over territory. In the lower photograph, you can see a fight between two young flap-necked chameleons. The winner (right) is wearing bright green. The loser has turned dark and is hiding behind the tree branch.

Baby chameleons are on their own as soon as they leave their eggs. There are no adults to take care of them. The babies must hide from birds, snakes, and even other chameleons that will try to eat them. They must also find water and food for themselves. (The little chameleon in the top photograph is swallowing a drop of water that it got from a leaf.)

The young chameleons already know how to use their long tongues to catch insects.

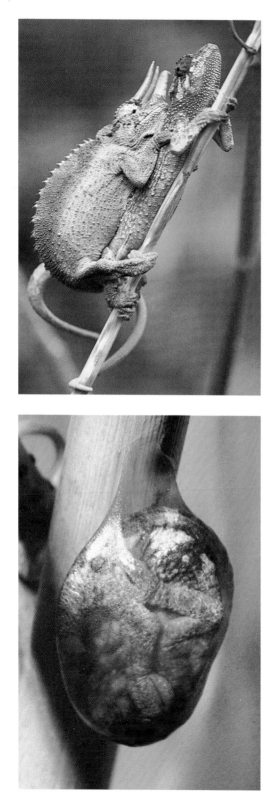

Most chameleon babies hatch out of eggs buried in the ground. A few come into the world in a different way. Some species, such as the Jackson's chameleon (shown here), produce young that are born alive and completely developed.

Jackson's chameleon is a three-horned species that lives in the high mountains of East Africa. In this cool climate, eggs buried in the ground might not be able to develop. After mating (upper left), the female Jackson's chameleon keeps her young inside her body until they have completed their growth.

Baby Jackson's chameleons are born, not on the ground, but in the trees. Each one comes out of the female's body enclosed in a transparent skin, or membrane (lower left). This thin covering is sticky and clings to leaves and branches. The tiny baby, only 1½ inches (4 centimeters) long, struggles out of the membrane.

A newly born Jackson's chameleon can climb over leaves and branches with ease. Its three horns are already growing on its head (opposite). The little lizard is ready to face the world on its own.

41

Brookesia spectrum

A Jackson's chameleon doesn't leave the trees even to give birth. But there are a few kinds of chameleons that are almost never found in trees. These lizards belong to a group called stump-tailed chameleons.

Stump-tailed chameleons live on the island of Madagascar, off the eastern coast of Africa. They spend most of their time on the ground or in low-growing bushes. Their short tails are not prehensile.

Many stump-tailed chameleons do not have the bright colors of their relatives that live in trees. These small lizards often match the colors of dry leaves (above). Their bodies are also shaped something like leaves. These features make them difficult to see amid the brush on the forest floor (opposite).

Chamaeleo wiedersheimi

People often use the word *chameleon* to refer to a person who is very changeable. A human "chameleon" is someone who goes through frequent changes in moods or states of mind. Real chameleons, as we have seen, change their colors frequently under the influence of their moods and their environments. The female chameleon shown on this page is not very happy about posing for her photograph. Her bright spots and her open mouth express her bad mood.

A chameleon's color changes are fascinating, but there are many other reasons to admire these little lizards. Now that you have been introduced to chameleons, you can appreciate all their amazing features.

GLOSSARY

anole: a slender, quick-moving lizard native to South and Central America and the southeastern part of the United States. Although they are sometimes called American chameleons, anoles are not members of the chameleon family.

binocular vision: a form of vision in which both eyes see the same image. Many birds and other animals with eyes on the sides of their heads see a separate image with each eye.

ectotherms: animals whose temperatures are controlled by their environments. Another word used to describe this condition is *cold-blooded.*

egg tooth: a special tooth that many young reptiles use to cut through their egg shells. After the reptile hatches, its egg tooth falls off.

embryos: animals in an early state of development, before birth or hatching

endotherms: animals whose temperatures are controlled by their internal body systems. Another word used to describe this condition is *warm-blooded.*

hormones: chemicals produced in an animal's body that regulate various bodily functions and activities

hyoid bone: a small piece of cartilage

in a chameleon's mouth that serves as a resting place for the folded-up tongue

keratin: the material that makes up the horny outer layer of a reptile's skin

melanin: a pigment that produces black or brown colors in animals or plants

melanophores: pigment cells that contain melanin

molt: to shed the outer layer of skin

pigments: materials in the cells of animals and plants that produce different colors

predator: an animal that kills and eats other animals

prehensile: capable of grasping an object, especially by wrapping around it

prey: animals that are killed and eaten by predators

reptiles: members of the scientific class Reptilia, including lizards, snakes, crocodiles, turtles, and tuataras. All reptiles have bodies covered with scales or bony plates.

Chamaeleo parsonii is a large chameleon that lives in Madagasgar. Its average length is about 22 inches (about 55 centimeters).

INDEX

ABOUT THE AUTHOR

Claudia Schnieper began her career as a book seller and is now a free-lance writer, editor, and translator. She is the author of several nature books for children, including the Carolrhoda Nature Watch books *On the Trail of the Fox* and *An Apple Tree through the Year.* Claudia lives with her husband, Robert, various cats and dogs, and a parrot in an old farmhouse near Lucerne, Switzerland.

ABOUT THE PHOTOGRAPHER

Max Meier is a free-lance photographer who specializes in photographing animals. When he is not busy taking pictures of spiders, frogs, and chameleons, he works in the Veterinary Hospital in Zurich, Switzerland. Max has published several animal books for children and an adult book on amphibians and reptiles. He makes his home in Zurich.